acropolis museum
short guide

text
Dimitrios Pandermalis
Alexandros Mantis
Alkestis Choremi
Christina Vlassopoulou
Stamatia Eleftheratou

editorial
Stamatia Eleftheratou

translation
Angeliki Kosmopoulou

april 2011

contents

The first Museum of the Acropolis was established in a cavity of the hill opposite the Parthenon in 1865. This museum never accommodated the antiquities of the Acropolis in a satisfactory manner, despite successive additions built on to it. Today, the new Museum, ten times larger in size than the original, provides a safe haven for the masterpieces of the Acropolis and ensures the prominence they deserve. This is achieved with ideal interior atmospheric conditions, natural lighting, as well as easy visitor access, panoramic views and superior layout of the exhibition areas.

In the international architectural tender of 2001, the winning proposal was submitted by the Swiss architect Bernard Tschumi, Dean of the School of Architecture of the University of Columbia, New York, with the Greek architect Michalis Photiadis. Their design aptly met the needs of erecting a new building with respect to the underlying excavation site, as well as providing visual contact between the Parthenon Hall and the temple itself.

Excavations carried out at the site of the new Museum unearthed an important part of the ancient city of Athens, featuring many architectural phases and thousands of finds that provided valuable insight into everyday activities, as well as in the peculiarities encountered in life under the towering form of the Acropolis. The final preparation of the archaeological excavation to receive visitors and the construction of a dedicated exhibition area are expected to be completed soon. Until that time, visitors to the Acropolis Museum will be provided with a glimpse of the excavation through the openings and glass floors at the ground level of the Museum.

The new Acropolis Museum aspires to give visitors the opportunity to discover for themselves the unsurpassed quality of the masterpieces of ancient Athens that have fascinated western civilization. Visitors can enjoy, for the first time, the entire sculpted decoration of the Parthenon as it was on the ancient building, even if this is achieved through combining original sculptures with copies of those in the British Museum.

The demanding yet fascinating task of the mounting of the Museum's exhibition program was undertaken by archaeologists Dimitrios Pandermalis, Alexandros Mantis, Alkestis Choremi, Christina Vlassopoulou, Stamatia Eleftheratou and architects Iordanis Dimakopoulos and Alexandros Xenakis.

A detailed guide to the museum will be available shortly, thanks to the concerted efforts of the archaeologists-authors of the present short guide.

Dimitrios Pandermalis
President of the Acropolis Museum

Clay spindle whorls, dedications of women to the Sanctuary of the Nymphe. 6th and 5th cent. BC

the gallery of the slopes of the acropolis

The first gallery of the Museum houses finds from the slopes of the Acropolis. Its glass floor affords a view to the archaeological excavation, while the rise in the floor alludes to the ascent to the Acropolis.

In antiquity, the slopes of the Acropolis constituted the transition zone between the city and its most famous sanctuary. This was the area where official and popular cults, as well as large and small sanctuaries existed alongside private houses.

The settlement

Among the sanctuaries, or at a slightly lower level, excavations brought to light parts of the urban fabric of ancient Athens and provided evidence of its almost uninterrupted habitation from the end of the Neolithic period (about 3000 BC) until late antiquity (6th century AD and later). Houses and workshops, roads and squares, wells and reservoirs as well as thousands of objects left behind by the local people in antiquity provide insight into the past. Most of the finds are made of clay, as objects made of other perishable materials have been lost to us, while the most valuable objects have been looted. Tableware and symposium vessels, cooking pots, perfume holders, cosmetics and jewelry containers, children's toys and others are included amongst these finds.

The sanctuaries

The slopes, caves and plateaus of the Acropolis hill were the settings in which gods, heroes and nymphs were worshipped.

The south slope was home to two of the most important sanctuaries of the city, those of *Dionysos Eleuthereus* and *Asklepios*. It was also the site of several other temples, smaller in size yet of great importance to the Athenians.

The temple of *Dionysos Eleuthereus* was the site of the *Great* or *City Dionysia*, one of the most important festivals in town, which took place in the beginning of spring (in the month Elaphebolion). It was from the cult of Dionysos, the god of wine, intoxication and ecstatic dance, that the theatre was born. On the slope above the sanctuary, the plays of the most important ancient Greek tragic and comic playwrights, Aeschylus, Sophokles, Euripides and Aristophanes, were performed for the first time.

The sanctuary and associated healing centre of **Asklepios** in Athens was founded on the south slope of the Acropolis, through the initiative of Telemachos, an Athenian citizen who, in 420/19 BC, brought a statue of the god from the great sanctuary at Epidaurus. In a stoa beside the sanctuary, patients lay in wait for their miraculous cure by the apparition of the god in their dreams. The numerous votive offerings, often with depictions of the body parts that the god healed, provide evidence of the great importance the god's cult had for the Athenians.

At a short distance from the sanctuary of Asclepios was a small open-air sanctuary dedicated to the **Nymphe,** who was the protectress of marriage and wedding ceremonies. There the Athenians dedicated the nuptial bath vases or *loutrophoroi*, as well as other votive offerings (perfume bottles, cosmetics and jewelry containers, spindle-whorls, symposium vases, figurines, female protomes and painted plaques). The *loutrophoroi* were luxury vases painted in the red or black figure technique. Their decorative motifs were related to marriage and reflected the style prevalent at the time. The earlier vases depicted wedding processions, animals and mythical creatures. These were enriched, later on, with themes and scenes from mythology, which were directly associated with the three-day long wedding festivities: the procession of women who carried the water for the nuptial bath in the *loutrophoroi*; the adornment of the bride; the meeting of the couple; the transfer of the newlyweds to the groom's house; and the offering of gifts to the bride.

The settlement: Terracotta Nike, possibly decorative element from the roof of a building (acroterion). 1st-3rd cent. AD

The south slope was also dedicated to the cults of the Nymphs and Pan, Aphrodite, Hermes and Isis. Aphrodite was worshipped in her capacity as *Pandemos* on the southwest slope and as *Ourania* on the north. Aphrodite Ourania was the protector of all kinds of unions, as that of marriage, while Aphrodite Pandemos was the protector of all Attic *demoi* (subdivisions of Attica).

The age-old cult of fertile nature developed at the temple of *Ge Kourotrophos* and *Demeter Chloe*, on the southwest slope. The local cult of the *Hero on Blaute (blaute = luxury sandal)* at the same site was probably associated with Aphrodite.

Three caves on the northwest slope were home to the cults of **Zeus**, **Apollo** and **Pan**. According to myth, **Apollo** had intercourse with Kreoussa, the daughter of King Erechtheus in the cave of the Acropolis. Their son, Ion, was the mythical ancestor of the Athenians. The swearing-in ceremony of the nine archons of the city was conducted in this cave. The cult of Pan was introduced at a later stage, after the battle of Marathon (490 BC), when the goat-like god led the Athenians to victory, creating widespread panic among the Persians. Finally, a cave on the south slope was home to the cult of the nymph **Aglauros**, daughter of Kekrops, the legendary king of Athens.

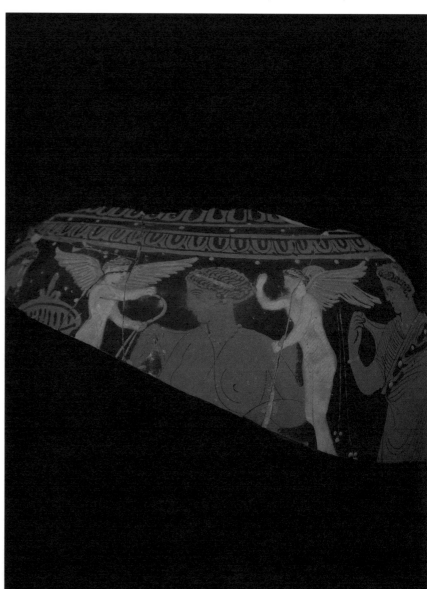

The Sanctuary of Nymphe: Fragment of a loutrophoros representing a bride crowned by Erotes. 4th cent. BC

The settlement: Maenads from the decoration of the clay lid of a jewel box (lekanis). 4th cent. BC

Votive eyes – offering to the Sanctuary of Asklepios. 350-300 BC

Relief slab from the facing of a base. Dionysos holds an amphora and kantharos. From the Sanctuary of Dionysos. Early 4th cent. BC

The Acropolis hilltop in the Mycenaean and Geometric period (16th – 8th century BC)

The flat open spaces atop the Acropolis were the seat of the Mycenaean ruler. In his palace, Athena *Polias* was worshipped as the patron goddess of the city. After the end of the Mycenaean civilization, in the 8th century BC, a small temple dedicated to Athena Polias was erected at the site of the palace that was, by then, in ruins. It is the temple mentioned by Homer, where the large bronze metal sheet in the form of a Gorgo head probably came from.

This temple and the succeeding ones built in the same area (*Archaios Naos, Erechtheion*) housed the sacred image of the goddess, made of olive tree wood (*xoanon*). The Athenians believed that the *xoanon* (cult image) had been sent by Zeus in the sky. That was the image dressed with the *peplos*, or veil, in the Panathenaic procession every four years.

Athena

The entire mythology of Athens and the history of the monuments on the Acropolis revolve around its patron deity. The Parthenon, the Erechtheion and the small temple of Athena Nike were dedicated to the goddess Athena in her various roles.

The prehistoric Athena was apparently a military deity and protected the Acropolis in her capacity as *Pallas*. Nevertheless as far back as in Homer's epics, Athena's war-like qualities were combined with another facet of her identity: Athena was also the goddess who weaved her own peplos. As *Ergane*, she protected carpenters, metalworkers and potters. As Athena *Nike*, a military deity, she fought in battle with her formidable aegis. Athena was also called *Parthenos* - and this capacity set her apart from her female nature, providing an explanation for her presence in battle and other exclusively male activities.

Athena also successfully competed against Poseidon for the domination of Attica. According to myth, Poseidon struck the rock with his trident and a source of salty water welled up. Athena won the battle when she offered the olive tree. From that time, she was linked with all aspects of urban life: religious, political, social and private.

The Acropolis in the Archaic period (7th – beginning of 5th century BC)

The Archaic period is characterized by the development of the city-state and the transition from aristocracy to tyranny and, eventually, democracy. It is also characterized by great achievements in the economy, art and intellectual life. In the early 6th century BC, the cult of Athena Polias on the Acropolis continued in her late-geometric temple. In 566 BC, the tyrant *Peisistratos* re-organized the *Panathenaia*, the greatest festival in honour of the goddess. It is possible that at that time, for reasons of political propaganda, a large temple was erected at the site to be occupied later by the Parthenon. It is the **Archaic Parthenon** or **Hekatompedos**, dedicated to the military aspect of Athena Parthenos, the patron divinity of the city.

The large poros pediment with the lions devouring a bull, flanked by two compositions, is attributed to this temple: on the one side, Heracles' wrestling with the wild Triton, and on the other side, the so-called three-bodied demon, that holds the symbols of the three elements of nature - water, fire and air in his hands. The figure of a lioness killing a calf, the horse protomes from a four-horse chariot and the relief spotted panthers are also linked to this temple.

A series of smaller buildings on the Acropolis, referred to as *oikemata* in the inscriptions, date from about the same time. In all likelihood, they were treasuries for the safekeeping of valuable votive offerings. Although their exact location on the hill has not been determined, evidence of their existence is provided by a series of architectural members and sculptures: *the Hydra Pediment, the Apotheosis of Herakles, The Troilos* or *Olive Tree Pediment* and the *Red Pediment*.

The abolition of tyranny in 508/7 BC was followed by Kleisthenes' reforms and the establishment of Democracy. At this time it was probably resolved that a new temple should be built at the site of the old (late geometric) temple of Athena Polias. This temple, referred to as the **Ancient Temple** by ancient sources, housed the goddess' age-old *xoanon*. The sculptures that decorated the pediments of the temple were fully carved out of Parian marble. One featured the *Gigantomachy*, the struggle of the revolted giants against the Olympian gods. Out of the entire composition, four figures have been reconstructed: the armed Athena defeating the giant *Engelados*; a giant sitting up on the ground; and two others lying down near the edge. Of the second pediment, fragments of a composition depicting a lion devouring a bull have survived. These sculptures are attributed to one of the two great Athenian sculptors at the time, *Antenor* or *Endoios*.

The pediment of the Archaic Parthenon or Hekatompedos. Around 570 BC

Chariot horses from a metope of the Hekatompedos. Around 570 BC

Votive offerings

From the time of Peisistratos onwards, the site of the Acropolis began to fill with votive offerings, dedicated to the goddess both as tokens of piety and as marks of financial and artistic development. These important offerings were mostly statues meant to please the goddess.

Votive offerings were used by the ancient Greeks to thank the gods for granting them a wish and frequently included a reference to the cost involved with the term *dekate*, that is one tenth of a specific source of income, or the term *aparche*, namely the first crop or the first earnings.

The type, material and size of the offerings reflected the time period, social status and financial state of the dedicant. On the Acropolis, statues and other expensive artefacts were commissioned by members of aristocratic families and wealthy professionals, manual workers, as well as women (such as washer woman and baker).

The inscriptions on the votive offerings sometimes included the names of the artists, some of whom are known to us through the ancient sources. The display of these names on statues, vases and small finds testifies to the important status enjoyed by artists and the public's appreciation of them.

The most distinctive offerings to the temple

of Athena on the Acropolis were the *Korai*, marble statues of young women. Carved in different sizes, they follow a strictly defined sculptural type, with an austere body posture. From the mid-6th century BC onwards, they are dressed in the fine linen chiton and heavier mantle-garments that set off their femininity more than the heavy woollen peplos. In one hand, they usually held an offering to the goddess, a pomegranate, wreath or bird, while with the other they lifted their pleated garment off the ground as they walked. The smile upon their face, the so-called archaic smile, hints at the demeanour of that period and conveys a sense of intense joy for their association with the goddess. Their garments bear bright painted decoration, while colour lights up their hair, face and jewellery.

In contrast to the large number of Korai, which is estimated to be in excess of 200, the number of marble male statues was rather small – a hardly surprising fact given the feminine nature of the deity worshipped on the Acropolis. A few statues of riders and scribes have survived.

Offerings also included marble reliefs depicting Athena and other gods, as well as mortals, like that of a potter.

The large bronze artefacts, of which only few have survived, were particularly

Detail of the Kore with pomegranate. 580-570 BC (Acr. 593)

expensive votive offerings, apparently commissioned by the wealthier citizens. Among the most expensive types of bronzes are the bronze cauldrons, large semi-spherical vases of the 8th and 7th century BC resting on tripods made of the same material. The rim, handles and shoulders of the vases were decorated with bronze statuettes of warriors, athletes, horses and mythical creatures, while the three-legged supports were covered by richly decorated bronze sheets.

Depictions of Athena or her symbols, like shields and owl figurines, were an integral part of the dedications. The Athena Promachos statue that stood on the Acropolis and was destroyed by the Persians in 480 BC was replicated by a number of statuettes. Other popular offerings included figurines of animals (horses, lions, dogs, bulls and wild boars) and mythical creatures (sphinxes, sirens and gorgons). Several bronze statues depicted athletes during the games – offerings on the occasion of a victory in a particular event.

The poorer citizens dedicated objects made of clay to Athena, mostly female statuettes bearing colourful painted decoration. Those seated on a throne depicted Athena, while the standing figures followed the marble type of the Kore. Other affordable offerings included terracotta protomes and figurines of riders and animals (dogs, birds, horses or cattle). Clay plaques depicted Athena either as Promachos, fully armed and resting one foot on a chariot, or as Ergane, seated and spinning. Others depicted deities, like Artemis, Apollo and Aphrodite, as well as heroes, such as Herakles.

The Kore *with the almond-shaped eyes.* 500 BC (Acr. 674)

Detail of the *Moschophoros* (calf-bearer). The statue dedicated by Rhombos, son of Palos, around 570 BC

Detail from a bronze figurine of Athena Promachos. End of 6th cent. BC

Terracotta figurine of a seated Athena. 500-480 BC

The Persian Wars and their vestiges on the Acropolis

The first two decades of the 5th century BC were marked by the defensive wars of the Greeks against the Persian invaders. The great victorious battles at Marathon, Salamis and Plataea were led by the Athenians, under generals Miltiades, Themistokles and Aristeides.

In 490 BC, following the victory at Marathon, the construction of a new marble temple began at the site of the Hekatompedos: the so-called Old Parthenon, which, however, was never completed, due to the Persian invasion in 480-79 BC.

In 480 BC the Persians set fire to the Acropolis and sacked its treasures. When they withdrew, the Athenians piously "buried" the remains of the sublime dedications and the colorful sculptures that adorned the destroyed temples in large pits.
Nevertheless, some vestiges of the Persian desecration deliberately remained visible, such as the column drums of the unfinished temple, built into the wall on the north slope of the Acropolis. The remains of the buildings and the broken votive offerings remained buried until the 19th century, when archaeological excavations brought them back to light. Many of them still retain traces of burning.

The year 480 BC is a milestone between Archaic and Early Classical art. The works of art created in the period until 450 BC express a new perception of life, following the shocking experience of the Persian Wars – an outlook reflected on the realistic rendering of the human body and the rendition of bold movement; the earnest facial expression with the fading of the Archaic smile; as well as the shift to simpler garments. This period is conventionally termed **Severe Style** and forms the prelude to Classical art.

The Kore most heavily damaged by the Persian invasion 510-500 BC (Acr. 1360)

Metopes of the south side of the Parthenon.

The Acropolis in the Classical period (mid-5th – second half of the 4th century BC)

It took the young Athenian Democracy a period of 30 years, from the Persian Wars to the mid-5th century BC, to reach its peak at the time of Perikles, a truly charismatic individual.

By instituting payment to state officials, he gave all Athenian citizens the opportunity to participate in public affairs for the first time. At the same time, he ensured that the state revenue increased, through the intensification of silver mining at the Lavrion mines. Moreover, he succeeded in transferring the allied treasure from Delos to Athens and ensured that a percentage amounting to 1/60 of the annual allied contribution was to be reserved for the Goddess on the Acropolis, who had taken on the protection of the fund. Through the institution of unprecedented democratic procedures, he obtained the approval of state bodies for the implementation of an ambitious plan for the reconstruction of the Acropolis.

Around 450 BC, the Sacred Rock had been cleared of the ruins left behind by the Persian invasion and was ready to receive new buildings. Perikles' building program involved, first of all, a magnificent temple for the Athena Parthenos, the deity embodying the power and prestige of the city of Athens, whose cult was perched at the highest spot of the rock. Moreover, he made provisions for a new temple of Athena as the goddess of victory, which stood next to the entrance to the Acropolis as a reminder of the victorious leadership of the city of Athens in the Persian Wars. The building program also included the creation of a monumental entranceway to the Acropolis, worthy of the grand Panathenaic procession that passed from that area. Finally, it also included the site with the ancient cults of the Acropolis rock and the ancient Athena Polias temple. It is at that site that the construction of the Erechtheion began in 421 BC. In 432 BC, before the completion of the Propylaea, the outbreak of a new war between Athens and Sparta, which lasted for 30 years, halted construction.

Nevertheless, the building program of Perikles, who had died in the beginning of the war, at the time between the hostilities, was completed. The buildings included in his program reflect the ideals of a society that cultivated the free spirit like no other: scientific investigation, political speculation, philosophical thinking and artistic production.

Block IV of the west frieze of the Parthenon. Horse rider and cavalry official.

The Parthenon

Perikles assigned the direction of all work on the **Parthenon** to the sculptor Pheidias and the program began in 447 BC. The temple, dedicated to Athena Parthenos, was constructed in 15 years and was the collaborative work of a large number of architects, sculptors, painters, coppersmiths, stoneworkers and others. The Parthenon was designed by architects *Iktinos* and *Kallikrates*, while for the carving of the sculptures Pheidias collaborated with his pupils *Agorakritos*, *Alkamenes* and other great artists. Pheidias himself created the gold-and-ivory statue of the armed goddess, which adorned the interior of the cella.

The architectural sculptures of the Parthenon, namely the metopes, frieze and pediments, were made of Pentelic marble and embellished with the addition of metal attachments and paint.

The 92 **metopes** were the first parts of the entablature to receive sculptural decoration. Each one reproduced a self-contained scene, usually including two figures. The subjects were taken from legendary battles and symbolized the victories of the Athenians against the Persians. The east side depicted the battle of the Olympian gods against the Giants, who tried to overthrow the order prevailing on Mt. Olympus (*Gigantomachy*). The west side presented the fight of Athenian youths against the Amazons, who threatened even the Acropolis (*Amazonomachy*). The theme of the south side was the fight of the Thessalian youths (Lapiths) against the Centaurs who attempted to abduct their women during a wedding celebration (*Centauromachy*). The north side illustrated the Sack of Troy (*Iliou Persis*).

The **pediments**, the triangular areas at the roof of the two temple fronts, carried sculptural compositions illustrating themes taken from Athenian mythology. The east pediment, above the temple entrance, depicted the birth of the goddess Athena from the head of her father, Zeus. The west pediment illustrated the dispute between Athena and Poseidon for the claim of the land of Attica – a legendary fight that resulted in Athena's victory.
In contrast to the mythological subjects of the metopes and pediments on the frieze, Pheidias chose to depict the Great Panathenaia, the greatest festival of the city on the **frieze** of the Parthenon. The festival took place every four years, lasted 12 days and included rituals, sacrifices, as well as athletic and musical contests.

The festivities culminated on the 28th day of the month - *Hekatombaion* in the heart of the summer – on Athena's birthday. On that day, a procession advanced to the temple of Athena Polias (the *Archaios Naos* that was later replaced by the Erechtheion) in order to hand over to the priests a new peplos for the old *xoanon* of the goddess. This procession unfolds over the 160 meters of continuous sculptural decoration of the Parthenon frieze.

The Parthenon frieze depicts 360 human and divine figures and more than 250 animals, mostly horses. Horsemen, chariots with *apobatai*, youths holding sacrificial oxen or rams, old *thallophoroi*, *hydriaphoroi* and other figures make up the composition. The procession starts at the southwest corner of the temple and, at that point, two distinct groups are formed. One proceeds to the west and north side, the other to the south. The two teams meet at the east side, where the delivery of the peplos takes place, under the watchful eye of the Olympian gods.

Block VI of the east frieze of the Parthenon. Poseidon, Apollo, Artemis.

North frieze of the Parthenon.

Block XXXIV of the north frieze of the Parthenon. A marshal directs the procession of horse riders.

The gathering of the gods on the east frieze of the Athena Nike Temple.

The Propylaia

The Propylaia, the monumental entrance to the Acropolis, were built in 437-432 BC following designs by the architect *Mnesikles*, in order to replace the earlier gateway.

The building consisted of a central section flanked by two wings at the sides. The main building featured five openings. The central opening was the widest one, to accommodate the passing through of the Panathenaic procession and sacrificial animals.

The north wing had an anteroom and a spacious hall known as the *Pinakotheke*. This was probably a recreation area with paintings on the walls and couches with tables, where visitors could rest. Works of art made by great sculptors, like the statue of *Hermes Propylaios* by Alkamenes, stood in the Propylaia.

The Temple of Athena Nike

Before the completion of the Propylaia, the outbreak of the Peloponnesian War between Athens and Sparta forced the Athenians to cease building activity. The Periklean building program was suspended and seemed to fade away when its leading exponent died in the great plague of 429 BC. However, when the situation settled for the first time, around 426 BC, the construction of the small marble temple of the *Athena Nike* began. The temple housed the wooden cult statue *(xoanon)* of the goddess, who held a pomegranate in one hand and a helmet in the other.

It was built on the bastion at the southwest end of the Acropolis, following the designs of architect Kallikrates, according to an ancient inscription. The temple followed the Ionian order and bore a sculpted frieze and pediments. Each side of the frieze featured a different theme. The east side illustrated the Assembly of the Olympian gods, the south side a battle between Greeks and Persians, while the other two sides depicted battles between Greeks. The pediments also carried sculpted decoration, probably representations of mythological battles, like the Gigantomachy and Amazonomachy.

The dangerous end of the bastion was blocked off by a marble balustrade, bearing a series of exquisite reliefs on the exterior illustrating the goddess Athena and winged Nikai who are either leading bulls to sacrifice or holding weapons and erecting trophies supporting Greek or Persian armament. Particularly noteworthy among them is the figure of the Nike adjusting her sandal.

The sculptures were carved by a team of many artists, led by Agorakritos.

The Erechtheion

The *Erechtheion* was built during the Peloponnesian War (421-415 and 410-406 BC) in order to replace the early temple of the Athena Polias, destroyed by the Persians. It owes its peculiar design to the natural irregularity of the bedrock, as well as to the need to protect and house the remains of ancient cults and the sacred spots associated with divine presence.

The building was divided into two parts. The eastern part was dedicated to Athena and housed her cult image *(xoanon)*. The western part was built on two levels. The upper one was dedicated to the cult of gods and local heroes– *Erechtheus, Hephaistos* and *Boutes,* Erechtheus' brother. The lower bore the vestiges of Poseidon's trident and incorporated the salted spring that gushed out from his blow on the rock, during his fight with Athena.

The building had two porches. The roof of the north porch was supported on six Ionic columns, while below its floor the Athenians pointed at the mark of the thunderbolt sent by Zeus to kill the legendary King Erechtheus. At the better-known south porch, the roof was supported by six statues of maidens

Nike adjusting her sandal. Slab from the Athena Nike balustrade. 410 BC

known as the Caryatids, instead of the typical columns. Below it stood the grave of Kekrops, another legendary King of Athens. A building inscription of the Erechtheion refers to the Caryatids simply as Korai (maidens), while the name Caryatids was assigned to them at a later time. Several interpretations about the Caryatids have been put forth. The most convincing of them supports the view that they constituted the visible portion of the grave of Kekrops and were the *choephoroi* who paid tribute to the glorious dead. The main building and the north porch were surrounded by a continuous Ionic frieze decorated with images of gods, heroes and mortals, in scenes related to the ancient cults of the Erechtheion. The figures were carved in Parian marble and affixed on slabs of grey Eleusinian limestone.

The Caryatids from the south porch of the Erechtheion. 420-415 BC

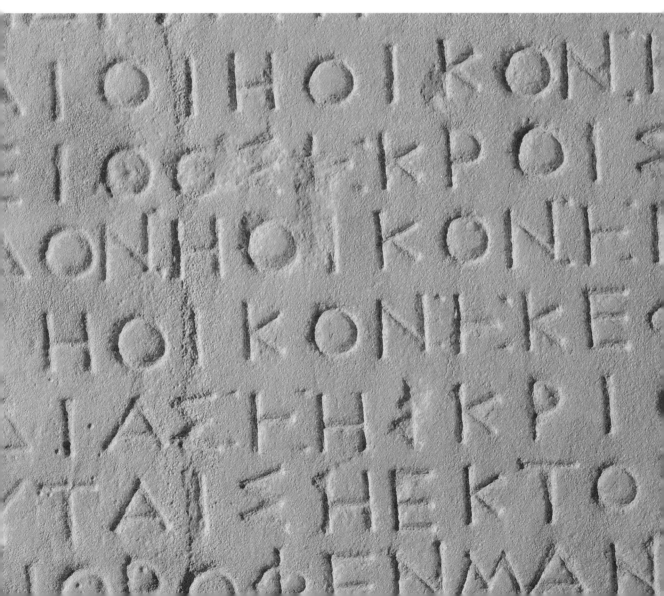

The Sanctuary of Artemis Brauronia

Artemis Brauronia was the goddess protecting expectant mothers and women in confinement. Her main sanctuary was located in the Attic *demos* of Brauron, in Attica. The sanctuary on the Acropolis was founded at the time of the tyrant *Peisistratos,* who originated from Brauron. The cella housed the wooden statue (*xoanon*) of the goddess, similar to the one in her Brauron temple. According to Pausanias, a second statue of Artemis, carved by Praxiteles, was added in the 4th century BC. The head of that statue is on display in the museum.

Votive offerings of the Classical period

Few of the precious offerings on the Acropolis, depicting gods, heroes and mortals from the legendary and historical past of Athens, have come to light. Among them stands the statue of *Prokne*, daughter of King Pandion of Attica, which illustrates the dramatic moment of her decision to kill her son, *Itys*, in order to punish her husband. The sculpture was a work by the famous artist Alkamenes. Other statues have survived in a fragmentary state, such as the statue of *Io* or *Kallisto* (the so-called *Barberini Suppliant),* another work by Alkamenes, or the fragment of the statue of the so-called *Aphrodite-Sosandra* by *Kalamis*. Unique is the famous relief depicting an Athenian trireme, possibly the sacred vessel *Paralos*. Another exquisite work is the portrait of Alexander, attributed to the sculptor *Leochares*. In some cases, only the relief bases of bronze statues have survived, like the *Atarbos* base depicting youths contesting the dance of *pyrrhiche* (war dance) and the athletes' base, attributed to the workshop of Lysippos.

The Acropolis and Athenian foreign policy

The 19th-century excavations on the Acropolis brought to light a number of honorary decrees and treaties with other city-states, often bearing a relief scene at the heading – the so-called document reliefs. The texts of these inscriptions refer to Athenian foreign policy, including the granting of honors and privileges and the signing of alliances and solidarity agreements.

Head of a youthful statue of Alexander the Great, attributed to the sculptor Leochares. 340-330 BC

Athenian decree honoring the Samians. The relief illustrates the patron deities of the two cities, Athena and Hera. 403 BC

The Acropolis in the Hellenistic Period (end of 4th – early 1st cent. BC)

In the course of the Hellenistic period, the Acropolis enjoyed the widespread recognition of the sovereigns of other states. Alexander the Great sent the shields from the Battle at Granicus to be put up on the Parthenon epistyle, while the Pergamene Kings erected on the Acropolis two quadrigas with royal statues and large mythological compositions. Eumenes II sponsored the erection of a luxurious stoa on the South Slope of the Acropolis.

The Acropolis in the Roman period (1st – 4th cent. AD)

From the erection of the Erechtheion to the end of antiquity, no new public buildings were erected on the Acropolis, with the exception of the small, circular temple of Rome and Augustus, whose architectural decoration quoted the Erechtheion. On the South Slope of the Acropolis, the Odeion was built in 160-170 AD, funded by Herodes Atticus.

Throughout the Roman period, the Acropolis retained the appearance it had in its heyday. It also preserved most of its dedications, unlike other Greek cities and sanctuaries, whose artistic treasures were plundered and transferred to Italy, mostly in order to adorn public buildings.

At the same time, a series of new dedications were added to the earlier ones. These were portraits of emperors, generals and other officials, portraits of philosophers, orators and priests, as well as images of individuals who benefited the city or distinguished themselves in athletic and other contests.

The Acropolis after the advent of Christianity

With the rise of Christianity in Athens, the Acropolis began to lose its significance. Toward the end of the 5th century AD, the operation of temples of the old religion ceased and the cult statues were pulled down. At that time, the bronze statue of Athena Promachos was taken to Constantinople and erected in the Forum of Constantine. The Parthenon was transformed into a Church of Holy Wisdom, while the Erechtheion became a church dedicated to the Virgin Mary. The ultimate predominance of Christianity was sealed in AD 529 by Justinian's decree prohibiting the teaching of law and philosophy in the city of Athens.

.

Portrait probably of Sauromates II, King of the Bosporan Kingdom. Around the end of the 2nd cent. AD

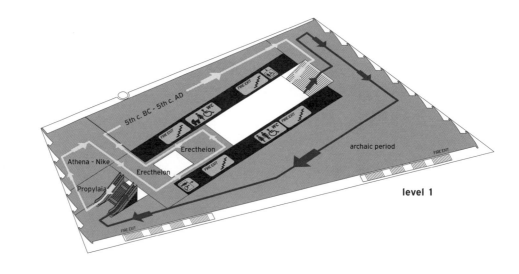

5th c. BC - 5th c. AD

Athena - Nike

Erectheion

Erectheion

Propylaia

archaic period

level 1

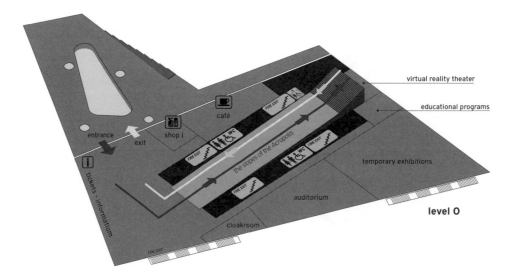

virtual reality theater

educational programs

café

entrance   exit   shop

the slopes of the Acropolis

temporary exhibitions

auditorium

tickets - information

cloakroom

level 0

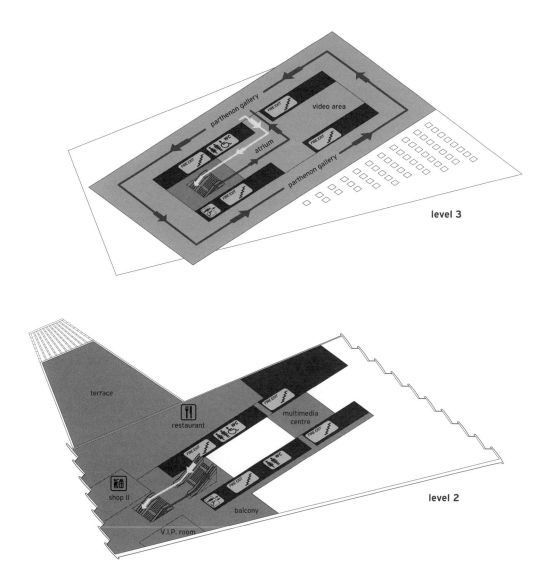

level 3

parthenon gallery

video area

atrium

parthenon gallery

level 2

terrace

restaurant

multimedia centre

shop II

balcony

V.I.P. room

μουσείο ακρόπολης
acropolis museum

**contributors: exhibition of the
acropolis museum**

Supervising Archaeologists
Pandermalis Dimitrios, Mantis Alexandros,
Vlassopoulou Christina, Choremi Alkestis,
Eleftheratou Stamatia

Communication Advisor
Dollis Niki

Archaeologists
Alexopoulou Alexandra, Vakoulis
Themistocles, Vaxovanou Athena, Vlahaki
Anna, Georgaca Vasiliki, Diamadidou
Katherine, Karra Irini, Kouveli Angelika,
Manoli Irini, Bakandritsou Andriani, Bizaki
Vasiliki, Bougatsou Ioanna, Papaloi Ioanna,
Petropoulou Theoni, Poulou Tatiana,
Charmalia Panagiota

Conservators
Maraziotis Dimitris, Paganis Georgos,
Agelopoulos Christos, Arbilias Panagiotis,
Vasiliadis Konstantinos, Gaki Amalia,
Gavrinioti Maria, Giatropoulis Iakobos,
Govatsou Eleni, Karteris Eleftherios,
Kilkis Dimitris, Koniaris Konstantinos,
Kousneref Jean-Mark, Maniadaki Eleni,
Lazarou Nansi, Magafas Dimitris, Mantzika
Georgia, Rachioti Vasiliki, Tzamourani
Roula, Tzempetzi Vasiliki, Farmaki Ioanna,
Fragou Evagelia, Hatzelenis Giorgos and
the painter Hiotis Antonis

Cast makers
Kagiorgis Theodoros, Baibas Antonis,
Argiris Giorgos, Liakopoulos Giorgos,
Magafas Ilias

Draughtsmen
Nika Panagiota, Nikas Alexandros

Photographers
Daniilidis Nikos, Tsangari Athina Rachel,
Kosintas Ilias, Spirou Despina

Technical Support
Lagios Alexandros, Mantas Paraskevas,
Kolokitha Antonia, Tabakakis Nikolaos

Security Supervisor
Mandas Athanasios

The final stages of work owe much to a number of
individuals: Anastasias Vasilis, Valsamis Lazaros,
Giannakena Varvara, Damianos Dimitris, Kallinikou
Garifalia, Karaba Eftihia, Katevas Fotis, Katsimardou
Panagiota, Kokkali Elissabet, Korosis Serafim,
Kirarinis Christos, Liolios Vasilis, Malliou Irini, Bardanis
Mihalis, Xanthouli Kalliopi, Panagiotopoulos Stelios,
Papathanasiou Eleni, Papaioannou Despina, Petinatou
Paraskevi, Pitsiri Panagiota, Sarri Maria, Stefanidis
Christos, Triantis Kostas, Fouseki Chrisa, conservators,
Trisbiotis Giannis, painter, Balli Rania, archaeologist

printing: KETHEA SCHEMA & CHROMA PRINTING UNIT